ABOUT THE AUTHOR

Neil Ardley has written a number of innovative nonfiction books for children, including *The Eyewitness Guide to Music*. He also worked closely with David Macaulay on *The Way Things Work*. In addition to being a well-known author in the fields of science, technology, and music, he is an accomplished musician who composes and performs both jazz and electronic music. He lives in Derbyshire, England, with his wife and daughter.

Project Editor Phil Wilkinson
Art Editor Peter Bailey
Photography Clive Streeter
Created by Dorling Kindersley Limited, London

Library of Congress Cataloging-in-Publication Data
Ardley, Neil.
The science book of air/by Neil Ardley.—1st U.S. ed.
p.   cm.
"Gulliver Books."
Summary: Simple experiments demonstrate basic principles of air and flight.
ISBN 0-15-200578-1
1. Air—Experiments—Juvenile literature. 2. Flight—Experiments—Juvenile literature. [1. Air—Experiments. 2. Flight—Experiments. 3. Experiments.] I. Title.
QC161.2.A74   1991
533'.6—dc20   90-36103

First U.S. edition 1991
H G F E D C

Printed in Belgium

THE SCIENCE BOOK OF AIR

Neil Ardley

Gulliver Books
Harcourt Brace & Company
San Diego   New York   London

What is air?

Air is invisible and you seldom feel it, except in a strong wind. But air is all around you. It presses on your body with great force. Because the air pressure is equal on the outside and inside of your body, you aren't aware of this force. Air pressure is very important. Many machines, such as jet engines, make use of the force exerted by air.

Moving along
A yacht uses the force of moving air blowing on its sails to travel through water.

How big are your lungs?
Your lungs can hold several liters of air. Blowing air into a bottle like this shows how much air your lungs can hold.

6

Pumping up

The pressure of the air in tires can support a bicycle or a huge truck. Here, air is supporting the weight of both the bicycle and its rider.

Jet power

When you let go of a balloon full of air, it shoots out of your hands as the air escapes from its neck. Jet engines work in a similar way.

Powerful pressure

Though it may seem odd, moving air has a lower air pressure (presses with less force) than still air. This is why aircraft and birds are able to fly. The moving air keeps them aloft and propels them through the sky.

⚠ This is a warning symbol. It appears within an experiment next to a step that requires caution. When you see this symbol, ask an adult for help.

Be a safe scientist
Follow all the instructions carefully and always use caution, especially with glass, scissors, matches, candles, and electricity.

Never put anything into your mouth or eyes. Remember to put out candles after using them and to unplug electrical equipment such as hair dryers.

Air is everywhere

Air is all around us. But you cannot see it, so how can you prove that it is actually there? This experiment shows that a jar that looks empty is in fact full of air, and that air has the power to hold things up.

You will need:

Funnel

Glass jar

Water

Modeling clay

Pencil

Make a tight seal with no holes.

1 Put modeling clay around the top of the jar so that the funnel is held in place in the middle.

2 Smooth down the modeling clay. Make sure there are no holes for air to escape through.

3 Pour the water slowly into the funnel.

You can color the water with food coloring so that you see it more clearly.

Air pushes on the water in the funnel and holds it there.

4 The water stays in the funnel.

Because the jar is full of air, there is no room for the water.

5 Using the pencil, make a hole through the modeling clay.

The air can leave the jar through the hole.

6 Now the water enters the jar.

Invisible support
There is air inside the large tires on this truck. The air supports the weight of the truck and its heavy load.

Hidden air

Why are wool clothes so warm to wear? Because air is trapped between them and your body. The air holds heat from your body, so that you are surrounded by a warm blanket of air. You can trap some air inside a wool glove and release it.

You will need:

Wool glove

Tank or bowl of water

Make sure the glove is dry.

Tangles of tiny wool threads trap the air inside the glove. This air stops heat from leaving your skin, and you stay warm.

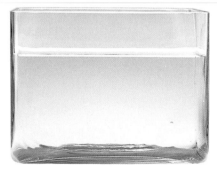

1 Fold the glove so that you can put your fingers around it.

2 Dip the glove in the water and squeeze. Air comes bubbling out of the wool!

Air lift

Air can support very heavy objects and even lift things off the ground. This simple experiment with a balloon shows you how you can topple a pile of heavy books using just the power of your breath.

Balloon

Books

1 Put the balloon on the edge of a table and pile the books on top.

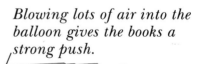

Blowing lots of air into the balloon gives the books a strong push.

2 Blow into the balloon. It lifts the books so that they topple over.

Traveling on air
A hovercraft uses air to lift itself in the same way that you used the air in the balloon to lift the books. It blows air under its hull so that it can travel just above the surface of the water.

Crushing air

How can you crush a plastic bottle without using your hands? Do it by warming the air inside to lower its pressure. The air outside the bottle presses harder than the air inside and crushes the bottle.

You will need:

Funnel   Warm water

Plastic screw-top bottle

3 Pour out the water and quickly put on the cap. Be sure the cap is tight.

2 Feel the bottle. Make sure that it gets warm.

4 Watch the bottle as it slowly collapses.

1 Work over a sink. Pour the warm water into the bottle.

A heavy load
Glassmakers use rubber suction cups to lift sheets of glass. Air pressing on the suction cups makes them grip the glass strongly.

Magic seal

Stop water pouring out of a glass as if by magic. You can use air pressure to seal the glass so that the water always stays inside—even when you turn the glass upside down!

Thin piece of cardboard   Glass   Water

Make sure there are no chips in the rim.

2 Slide the cardboard over the top of the glass, until it is touching the rim all the way around.

1 Work over a sink. Fill the glass with water.

Use one hand to hold the glass, the other to hold the cardboard.

The air outside presses on the cardboard with more force than the weight of the water inside.

3 Quickly but carefully turn the glass upside down.

4 Gently let go of the cardboard. It stays stuck to the glass, sealing the water inside.

Weighing air

Air seems to have no weight at all. But you can put some air on a balance and show that it is quite heavy.

You will need:

Two balloons

Thin piece of wood 0.5 m. (18 in.) long

Ruler

Tape

Balloon pump   Rubber band

Pencil

Two thumb-tacks

Thread

1 Use the ruler to find the center of the wood. Draw a line across the top.

2 Push a thumbtack into each side of the wood next to the line.

3 Tie the string to the middle of the rubber band, making two loops.

If the wood does not quite balance, put some modeling clay on one end.

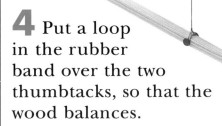

4 Put a loop in the rubber band over the two thumbtacks, so that the wood balances.

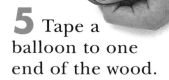

5 Tape a balloon to one end of the wood.

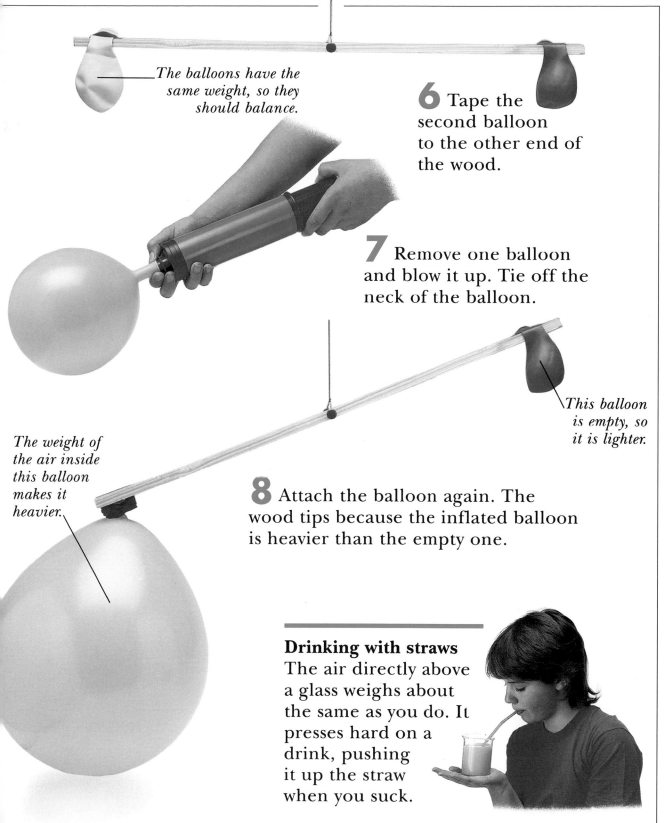

The balloons have the same weight, so they should balance.

6 Tape the second balloon to the other end of the wood.

7 Remove one balloon and blow it up. Tie off the neck of the balloon.

This balloon is empty, so it is lighter.

The weight of the air inside this balloon makes it heavier.

8 Attach the balloon again. The wood tips because the inflated balloon is heavier than the empty one.

Drinking with straws

The air directly above a glass weighs about the same as you do. It presses hard on a drink, pushing it up the straw when you suck.

Sky diver

Most things fall quickly when you drop them. The air does little to stop their fall. But air *can* slow down a falling object. You can make a parachute to find out how sky divers are able to leap out of a plane and float safely down to the ground.

You will need:

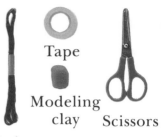

Handkerchief or any square of cloth

String

Tape

Modeling clay

Scissors

1 Cut four equal lengths of string.

If you do not have any tape, try tying the string to the cloth.

2 Tape one end of each piece of string to each corner of the cloth.

3 Fold the cloth and gather the loose ends of the strings together.

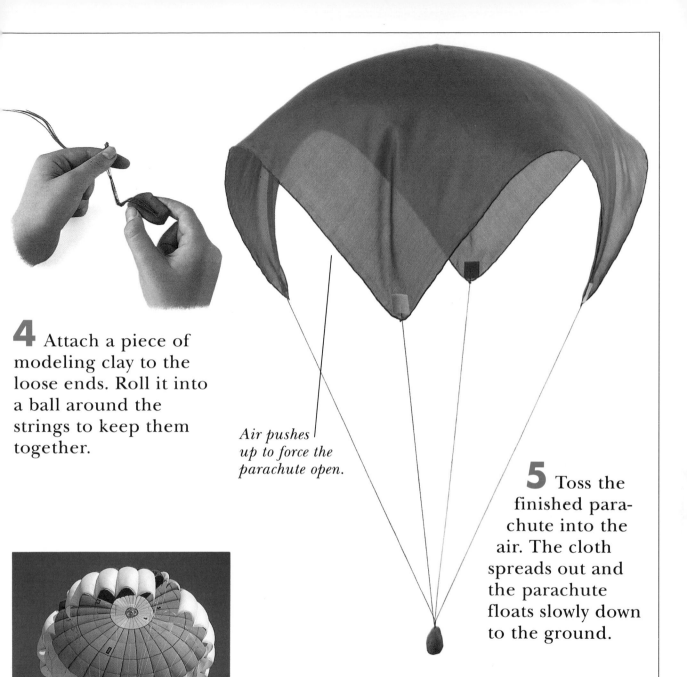

4 Attach a piece of modeling clay to the loose ends. Roll it into a ball around the strings to keep them together.

Air pushes up to force the parachute open.

5 Toss the finished para-chute into the air. The cloth spreads out and the parachute floats slowly down to the ground.

Why it works
Air pushes up against things as they fall. A parachute becomes very large as it opens, so a lot of air pushes up against it. Since the push is very strong it slows the fall of the sky diver.

What's in air?

By putting out a candle flame without blowing on it, you will see that air contains two gases and learn how air helps to provide us with energy.

You will need:

Modeling clay

Shallow dish   Candle   Water   Jar

1 Stick the candle to the dish with a piece of modeling clay.

2 Pour some water into the dish.

3 ⚠ Ask an adult to light the candle.

A narrow-necked jar works best.

4 ⚠ Place the jar over the candle

5 Watch the candle burn in the air inside the jar.

The candle flame uses up oxygen as it burns.

The flame goes out because the air in the jar now contains only nitrogen.

The air outside pushes water into the jar.

6 The water level gets higher and higher in the jar. The flame suddenly goes out, even though it is above the water.

Air and energy

Burning fuel provides most of the energy we use. Burning fuel in an engine powers this racing car. This process uses up some of the oxygen in the air.

Bizarre balloons

If you blow air between two hanging balloons, what will happen? You might expect them to move apart, but this experiment will show you how strangely moving air can behave.

You will need:

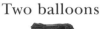

Two balloons

Balloon pump

Thread

Drinking straw

1 Blow up the two balloons to the same size. Tie each neck in a knot.

2 Hang the balloons on some thread so that they are a short distance apart.

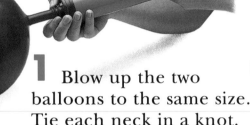

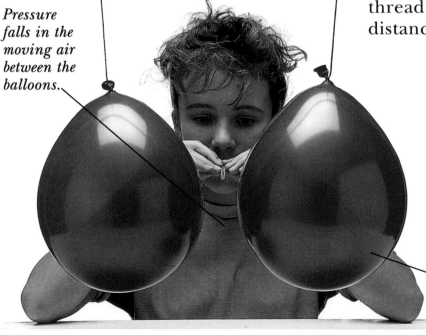

Pressure falls in the moving air between the balloons.

3 Using the straw, blow air between the balloons. They are not blown apart, but instead move together!

Still air at higher pressure pushes the balloons together.

20

Lights out

It's easy to blow out a candle with a puff of air. If you put a round object in the way, will it stop the air from blowing out the candle? Surprise yourself with the strange behavior of moving air.

Can

Candle

Drinking straw

Modeling clay

Shallow dish

Use the clay to attach the candle to the dish.

1 Place the can beside the candle and dish.

Point the straw at the side of the can away from the candle.

2 ⚠ Ask an adult to light the candle. Point the straw at the can as shown.

3 Blow through the straw. The stream of air travels around the can and blows out the candle flame!

The moving air is at lower pressure than the still air. The still air pushes low-pressure moving air around the can and toward the candle.

Air lift

How can you make a Ping Pong ball hover in midair without any visible support? Make a simple blowpipe and use it to blow air around the ball. See how the moving air does not blow the ball away, but gives it support.

You will need:

Empty spool

Flexible drinking straw

Four push-pins

Modeling clay

Ping Pong ball

1 Push the straw through the hole in the middle of the spool.

Clay holding pins

Pushpins

3 Put four small pieces of modeling clay on the upper end of the spool and push in four pins.

2 Smooth modeling clay around the straw so that it is fixed to the spool.

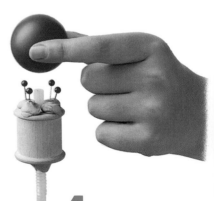

4 Place the ball on the pins.

5 Blow through the straw. Watch as the ball is lifted in the air and hovers above the spool.

Air moving around the ball has low pressure. There is unmoving air at higher pressure under the ball, and this supports the ball.

6 Tilt the spool and the ball should stay in midair above it.

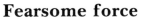

Fearsome force
A tornado destroys everything in its path. Air whirls at very high speed inside the tornado. Its pressure falls, and outside air rushes in and rises. The rushing air can lift heavy objects into the air and carry them away.

Flying wing

How do airplanes and gliders fly? You can find the answer by building a model wing and making it rise in the air. This will show you how moving air enables aircraft and birds to fly.

You will need:

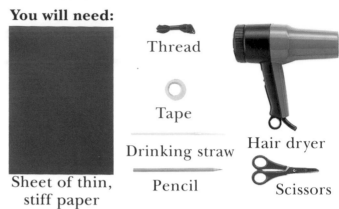

Thread

Tape

Drinking straw

Hair dryer

Pencil

Scissors

Sheet of thin, stiff paper

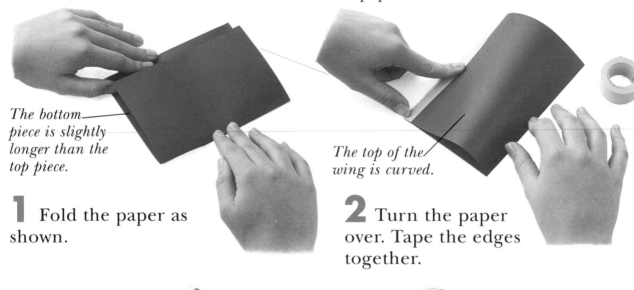

The bottom piece is slightly longer than the top piece.

The top of the wing is curved.

1 Fold the paper as shown.

2 Turn the paper over. Tape the edges together.

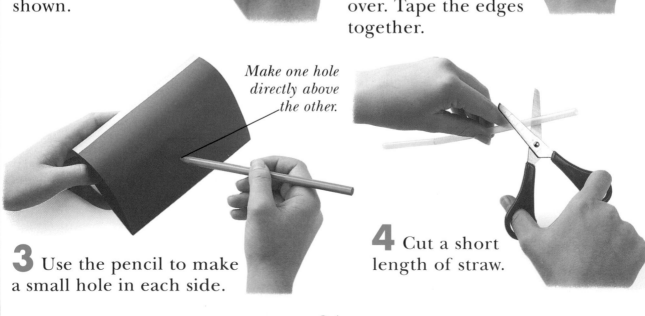

Make one hole directly above the other.

3 Use the pencil to make a small hole in each side.

4 Cut a short length of straw.

5 Push the piece of straw through the holes in the wing. Fix it in place with tape.

6 Push the thread through the straw.

Move the hair dryer in nearer to make the wing rise.

The curve makes air above the wing move aside. Air pressure above the wing falls as the air moves.

7 Tie the thread to some supports so the wing can move up and down. Turn on the hair dryer to a cool setting and blow air over the wing. The wing will rise up the thread.

Still air under the wing has a higher pressure and lifts the wing.

Gliding
A glider wing has the same shape as the wing you have just made, giving it the lift it needs to stay in the air.

Paper plane

Why are fast aircraft like the Concorde shaped differently from other planes? Building a plane from a single sheet of paper will show you how the world's fastest airliner flies.

You will need:

Sheet of thin, stiff paper

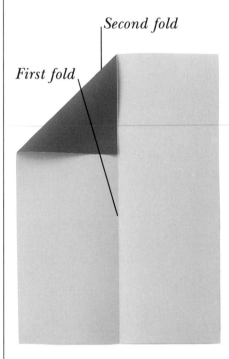

First fold

Second fold

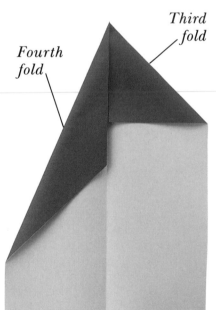

Fourth fold

Third fold

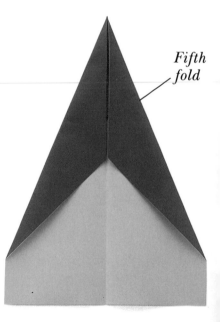

Fifth fold

1 Fold the paper lengthways down the middle. Open it. Then fold one top corner into the middle.

2 Fold in the other top corner. Then take the second fold and fold it in to the middle of the paper.

3 Fold the third fold in to the middle of the paper to create a pointed shape with the edge of the paper showing at the bottom.

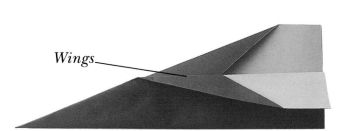

Wings

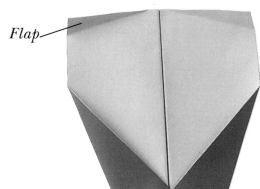

Flap

4 Fold the two halves of the paper together. Then fold out the two top edges to make two triangular wings. Push up the top of each wing to give a slight curve.

5 Fold up small flaps on the tail of the plane.

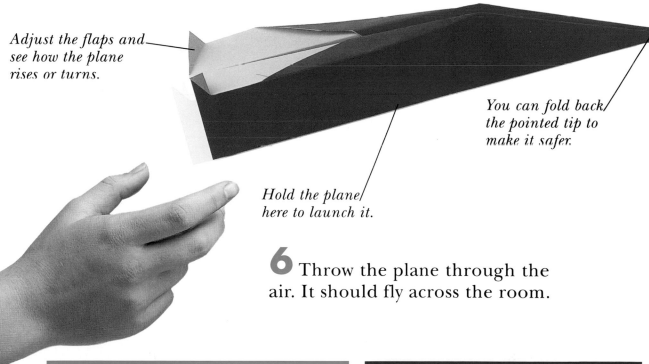

Adjust the flaps and see how the plane rises or turns.

You can fold back the pointed tip to make it safer.

Hold the plane here to launch it.

6 Throw the plane through the air. It should fly across the room.

Darting through the air
The Concorde is the world's fastest airliner. Shaped like a dart, it can cut through the air at high speed. Flaps on the wings control its flight.

Jet balloon

How do aircraft fly around the world at great speed? They use the power of air to push them through the sky. The engines in airliners and in some special high-speed cars produce a powerful stream or jet of air that makes them move. This is why they are called jet engines. You can use this same power to make a balloon fly across a room.

You will need:

String

Tape

Balloon

Drinking straw

Balloon pump

1 Push the string through the straw.

2 Stretch the string across the room. Attach two pieces of tape to the straw.

3 Use the pump to blow up the balloon.

4 Hold the neck tightly and attach the pieces of tape to the balloon.

A fast stream of air comes from the neck, pushing the balloon forward.

5 Let go of the balloon. It rushes along the string at high speed.

Fast mover

This high-speed car is the world's fastest vehicle. It has a jet engine. It produces a very powerful stream of air that pushes the car forward very quickly.

Picture credits
(Picture credits abbreviation key: B=below, C=center, L=left, R=right, T=top)

Pete Gardner: 6BR,7TL; Hoverspeed Ltd: 11BL; The Image Bank: 6TL; P J May: 23BL; Adrian Meredith: 27BR; Science Photo Library/Jerrican Gontier: 12BC; Stockphotos: 7CR; Thrust Cars Ltd: 29CL; Jerry Young: 25CB; Zefa: 9BL, 17BL, 19BR

Picture research Cynthia Hole

Title page photography Dave King

Dorling Kindersley would like to thank Claire Gillard for editorial assistance and Mark Regardsoe for design assistance; Mrs Bradbury, the staff and children of Allfarthing Junior School, Wandsworth, especially Joe Armstrong and Melanie Best; Nadia Agadia, Katie Martin, Tara Mathurin, and Kate Whiteway.